Mastering AI and Generative AI: From Learning Fundamentals to Advanced Applications

TABLE OF CONTENTS

Part 1: The World of Artificial Intelligence

Part 3: Generative AI Across Domains

- Deep Dream and Neural Style Transfer: Reimagining the World Through Artistic Filters

- Building Realistic Images and Videos: Exploring Cutting-Edge Generative Models

- Applications of Image/Video Generative AI: From Art Creation to Special Effects in Films

Part 4: The Future Landscape of Generative AI

Part 1: The World of Artificial Intelligence

Chapter 1: Unveiling Artificial Intelligence

Welcome to the fascinating world of Artificial Intelligence (AI)! In this chapter, we'll embark on a journey to understand what AI truly is, explore its diverse subfields, and delve into the philosophical questions it raises.

1.1 What is AI and What Can It Do?

Imagine machines that can learn, reason, and solve problems — that's the essence of Artificial Intelligence. It's the field of computer science dedicated to creating intelligent systems that can mimic human cognitive abilities.

But AI isn't a monolithic entity. It encompasses a rich tapestry of subfields, each tackling specific aspects of intelligence:

- **Machine Learning (ML):** This subfield empowers machines to learn from data without explicit programming. Think of a self-driving car learning to navigate by analyzing driving data.

- **Deep Learning (DL):** A powerful subset of ML inspired by the structure and function of the human brain. Deep learning algorithms, often called neural networks, excel at tasks like image recognition and speech understanding.

. **Natural Language Processing (NLP):** This subfield bridges the gap between humans and machines by enabling computers to understand and process human language. NLP fuels chatbots, machine translation tools, and sentiment analysis.

. **Computer Vision:** As the name suggests, this subfield equips machines with the ability to "see" and interpret the visual world. It allows for object recognition, image classification, and even autonomous robots navigating their environment.

1.2 A Historical Journey Through AI

The quest to create intelligent machines has a long and captivating history. From the early philosophical musings of Alan Turing to the development of the first neural networks, AI researchers have constantly pushed the boundaries of what's possible. Let's take a quick trip down memory lane:

- **Early Days (1950s-1960s):** The birth of AI! Pioneering figures like Alan Turing laid the groundwork for the field with concepts like the Turing test, a measure of a machine's ability to exhibit intelligent behavior equivalent to, or indistinguishable from, that of a human.

- **The Rise and Fall of AI (1960s-1980s):** Initial optimism was dampened by limitations in computing power and the complexity of AI problems. This period is often referred to as "AI Winter".

. **The Comeback (1990s-Present):** With advancements in computing power and algorithms, AI research experienced a resurgence. Subfields like machine learning flourished, leading to groundbreaking applications in various domains.

1.3 Can Machines Think? The Philosophical Debate

The very nature of AI raises profound philosophical questions. Can machines truly think and be intelligent? Here are some key perspectives in this ongoing debate:

- **Strong AI:** This school of thought believes that machines can achieve true intelligence, potentially surpassing human capabilities in the future.

- **Weak AI:** This view suggests that AI is simply a tool for simulating intelligent behavior, but lacks genuine consciousness or understanding.

- **The Turing Test:** Proposed by Alan Turing, this test asks whether a human judge can distinguish between conversation with a human and a machine. Passing the Turing test would be a strong argument for machine intelligence.

As we delve deeper into AI, these philosophical questions will continue to challenge us, prompting us to consider the very nature of intelligence itself.

This chapter has provided a foundational understanding of AI, its subfields, and the historical and philosophical landscape surrounding it. In the next chapters, we'll delve deeper into the exciting world of Generative AI!

Chapter 2: Mastering Machine Learning Fundamentals

Welcome to the world of Machine Learning (ML), a subfield of AI that empowers machines to learn from data! In this chapter, we'll unpack the core concepts of ML, explore different algorithms, and shed light on how to measure their success.

2.1 Learning from Experience: Unveiling Supervised vs. Unsupervised Learning

Imagine a student learning from a teacher's guidance — that's the essence of supervised learning. In this approach, we provide the machine with labeled data sets. Think of images labeled as "cat" or "dog." The machine analyzes these examples, learns the patterns, and can then predict labels for new, unseen data.

On the other hand, unsupervised learning is like letting a student explore on their own.

Here, the data is unlabeled, and the machine's task is to uncover hidden patterns and structures within it. For instance, an unsupervised algorithm might group similar customer purchase data into clusters, revealing hidden buying trends.

2.2 A Powerful Toolbox: A Compendium of Machine Learning Algorithms

The world of ML boasts a diverse collection of algorithms, each excelling at specific tasks. Here's a glimpse into some popular ones:

- **Linear Regression:** A workhorse for predicting continuous values, like house prices based on size and location.

- **Decision Trees:** Imagine a flowchart for making decisions. Decision trees use a series of yes/no questions to classify data points.

- **Support Vector Machines (SVMs):** These algorithms excel at finding the best separation line between different categories in data.

- **K-Nearest Neighbors (KNN):** This approach classifies data points based on the majority vote of their nearest neighbors in the training data.

As we delve deeper into AI, we'll encounter a powerful subset of ML algorithms called Deep Learning, which will be covered in the next chapter.

2.3 Data Wrangling: The Unsung Hero of Machine Learning

Before a machine can learn magic from data, that data needs some preparation – that's where data wrangling comes in. It's the art of cleaning, transforming, and organizing data to make it usable for machine learning models.

Think of a messy room before a party. Data wrangling is like tidying up the room, removing clutter (missing values), organizing furniture (fixing inconsistencies), and ensuring everything is spotless (handling errors) for the machine learning model to function at its best.

2.4 Measuring Success: A Look at Evaluation Metrics

So, how do we know if our machine learning model is actually learning anything? That's where evaluation metrics come in. These metrics provide a quantitative measure of a model's performance on unseen data.

Common metrics include:

- **Accuracy:** The percentage of predictions that are correct for a classification task.

- **Precision:** How often a positive prediction is actually correct.

- **Recall:** How often the model identifies all the relevant data points.

- **Mean Squared Error (MSE):** Measures the average squared difference between predicted and actual values for regression tasks.

By analyzing these metrics, we can fine-tune our models and ensure they are learning effectively.

Chapter 3: Delving Deep into Deep Learning Architectures

Get ready to dive deeper into the fascinating world of Deep Learning (DL)! This chapter will introduce you to the building blocks of DL – neural networks – and explore specific architectures that excel at different tasks.

3.1 Demystifying Neural Networks: The Building Blocks of Deep Learning

Inspired by the structure and function of the human brain, neural networks are the foundation of deep learning. These complex algorithms are composed of interconnected artificial neurons, which process information in layers.

Information flows through these layers, with each layer transforming the data and extracting higher-level features. The more layers a network has, the "deeper" it becomes, allowing it to learn increasingly complex patterns.

2.2 Convolutional Neural Networks (CNNs): Masters of Image Recognition

CNNs are a specialized type of neural network designed for image recognition and processing. They excel at tasks like identifying objects in a picture or classifying different types of medical scans.

CNNs leverage a specific architecture with convolutional layers that can automatically detect edges, shapes, and other visual features within an image, ultimately leading to accurate image classification.

2.3 Recurrent Neural Networks (RNNs): Capturing Sequences and Dependencies

Unlike CNNs that primarily deal with static images, Recurrent Neural Networks (RNNs) are adept at handling sequential data. RNNs excel at tasks that involve understanding the order or relationships between elements, such as language translation, speech recognition, and time series forecasting.

2.4 Deep Learning Frameworks: Tools for Building and Deploying Deep Learning Models

Building and training deep learning models can be computationally intensive. Thankfully, there are powerful software tools called deep learning frameworks that simplify the process. These frameworks provide pre-built functions, libraries, and optimization algorithms, allowing you to focus on designing and implementing your models.

Here are some popular deep learning frameworks:

- **TensorFlow:** An open-source framework developed by Google, offering flexibility and a wide range of capabilities.

- **PyTorch:** Another popular open-source framework known for its ease of use and dynamic computational graph.

- **Keras:** A high-level API that can be used on top of TensorFlow or other frameworks, offering a simpler interface for building models.

By leveraging these frameworks, researchers and developers can create and deploy complex deep learning models for various applications.

Chapter Summary

In this part, we explored the fundamental concepts of Artificial Intelligence and its subfield, Machine Learning. We learned about different learning paradigms, popular algorithms, and the crucial role of data preparation. We then delved into the exciting world of Deep Learning, uncovering the power of neural networks and the specialized architectures like CNNs and RNNs. Finally, we discovered the valuable tools – deep learning frameworks – that empower us to build and deploy these powerful models.

As we move forward, we'll be applying these concepts to understand the fascinating realm of Generative AI and its transformative potential.

Chapter 3: Delving Deep into Deep Learning Architectures

Welcome to the exciting world of Deep Learning! In this chapter, we'll unveil the intricate structures known as neural networks, the fundamental building blocks of deep learning. We'll then explore specialized architectures like Convolutional Neural Networks (CNNs) and Recurrent Neural Networks (RNNs) designed to excel at specific tasks. Finally, we'll introduce you to powerful tools called deep learning frameworks that simplify the process of building and deploying these complex models.

3.1 Demystifying Neural Networks: The Brains Behind the Machine

Imagine a network of interconnected artificial neurons, loosely inspired by the structure and function of the human brain. This is the essence of a neural network! These networks consist of layers of interconnected nodes that process information by passing signals through them. By adjusting the connections between these nodes (weights), we can train neural networks to learn complex patterns from data.

Here's a breakdown of the key components:

- **Neurons:** The processing units of the network, receiving input signals, applying mathematical functions, and sending output signals to other neurons.

- **Activation Functions:** Mathematical functions applied to the weighted sum of inputs within a neuron, introducing nonlinearity and allowing the network to learn complex relationships.

- **Layers:** Groups of interconnected neurons that process information hierarchically, with each layer building upon the previous one.

Through a training process called backpropagation, neural networks learn to adjust the weights between neurons to minimize errors and improve their performance on a specific task.

3.2 Convolutional Neural Networks (CNNs): Masters of Image Recognition

Not all neural networks are created equal! Convolutional Neural Networks (CNNs) are a specialized type of deep learning architecture designed specifically for image recognition and processing tasks.

Here's what makes CNNs exceptional for images:

- **Convolutional Layers:** These layers apply filters that scan the image, extracting features like edges and shapes. By stacking convolutional layers, CNNs can learn increasingly complex features.

- **Pooling Layers:** These layers downsample the data, reducing its dimensionality while preserving essential information. This helps control overfitting and improves computational efficiency.

CNNs have revolutionized image recognition tasks like object detection, image classification, and even medical image analysis.

3.3 Recurrent Neural Networks (RNNs): Capturing Sequences and Dependencies

While CNNs excel at images, Recurrent Neural Networks (RNNs) are built to handle sequential data, where the order of elements matters.

Here's how RNNs capture sequence information:

- **Internal Memory:** RNNs have a built-in loop that allows them to store information from previous inputs and use it to influence their processing of current inputs. This "memory" is crucial for understanding the context of sequential data.

This makes RNNs ideal for tasks like:

- **Text Generation:** RNNs can analyze large amounts of text data and learn the patterns of language, allowing them to generate new text that mimics the style and structure of the training data.

- **Machine Translation:** RNNs can translate text from one language to another by considering the order of words and their relationships within a sentence.

. **Speech Recognition:** RNNs can translate spoken language into text by analyzing the sequence of sounds and their context within an utterance.

3.4 Deep Learning Frameworks: Tools for Building and Deploying Deep Learning Models

Building and training deep learning models can be computationally intensive. Thankfully, there are powerful software tools called deep learning frameworks that simplify the process.

These frameworks provide pre-built functions, libraries, and optimization algorithms, allowing you to focus on designing and implementing your models.

Here are some popular deep learning frameworks:

- **TensorFlow:** An open-source framework developed by Google, offering flexibility and a wide range of capabilities.

- **PyTorch:** Another popular open-source framework known for its ease of use and dynamic computational graph.

- **Keras:** A high-level API that can be used on top of TensorFlow or other frameworks, offering a simpler interface for building models.

By leveraging these frameworks, researchers and developers can create and deploy complex deep learning models for various applications, pushing the boundaries of what's possible with AI.

This chapter has equipped you with the foundational knowledge of deep learning architectures and introduced you to the valuable tools that empower us to build and deploy these powerful models. As we move forward, we'll delve deeper into the fascinating world of Generative AI and explore how it leverages these deep learning architectures to create entirely new data.

Part 2: The Power of Generative AI

Chapter 4: Generative Magic: Unveiling the Potential

Welcome to the realm of Generative AI, where machines don't just learn, they create! In this chapter, we'll unveil the magic behind generative models and explore the vast spectrum of applications that are transforming our world.

4.1 Understanding Generative Models: From Imitation to Innovation

Imagine an artist inspired by a museum exhibit, but instead of replicating a piece, they create an entirely new artwork. That's the essence of generative models. These AI models analyze existing data and use that knowledge to generate entirely new, yet similar, data.

For instance, a text generative model trained on a massive corpus of novels could create a new story in the same genre. An image generative model could use photographs to create never-before-seen pictures that retain realistic details.

4.2 A Spectrum of Applications: The Limitless Potential of Generative AI

The applications of generative AI are as diverse as human imagination itself. Here's a glimpse into some exciting possibilities:

- **Text Generation:** Imagine AI-powered chatbots that can hold engaging conversations, or creative writing tools that spark new ideas for novelists and poets.

- **Image Synthesis:** Generative models are revolutionizing the world of design, creating realistic product mockups, or even generating artistic styles based on famous painters.

- **Music Creation:** AI can compose new music pieces, mimicking the style of different genres or artists, or even personalizing soundtracks for films and video games.

Beyond these, generative AI has the potential to impact various fields like drug discovery, materials science, and even scientific research by creating new molecules or simulating complex systems.

Chapter 5: Generative Adversarial Networks (GANs): A Deep Dive

Among the different types of generative models, Generative Adversarial Networks (GANs) have captured the imagination of researchers and the public alike. This chapter delves into the fascinating world of GANs, exploring their unique architecture and the challenges of training them effectively.

5.1 The Intrigue of GANs: A Competitive Dance Between Creation and Critique

Imagine two AI systems locked in an eternal artistic duel. That's the core idea behind GANs! A **generator** model continuously strives to create new, realistic data (like images or text). But its work is constantly scrutinized by a **discriminator** model, whose job is to distinguish the generated data from real data.

Through this ongoing competition, the generator learns to improve its creations, while the discriminator becomes a better critic. This adversarial training process pushes both models to excel, ultimately leading to the generation of high-quality, realistic data.

5.2 Unveiling the Math Behind GANs: Training Loss Functions and Optimization Techniques

While the concept of GANs might seem intuitive, the underlying mathematics can be quite complex. These models rely on specialized **loss functions** that measure how well the generator is fooling the discriminator, and vice versa. By optimizing these loss functions using sophisticated algorithms, the GANs are "trained" to improve their performance over time.

5.3 Taming the GAN Beast: Challenges and Best Practices for Effective Training

Training GANs can be a delicate dance. Finding the right balance between the generator and discriminator is crucial. If the generator is too weak, the discriminator will always win. If it's too strong, the discriminator might lose its ability to distinguish real from fake.

Researchers have developed various techniques to address these challenges, such as careful network design, gradient penalty methods, and progressive training strategies. By employing these best practices, we can unleash the full potential of GANs and unlock new frontiers in generative AI.

This part has provided a foundational understanding of generative AI and the power of generative models. We've explored the exciting potential of Generative Adversarial Networks and peeked into the complexities of their training process. In the next chapters, we'll delve deeper into specific applications of generative AI across various domains.

Part 3: Generative AI Across Domains

Welcome to the thrilling realm where machines not only mimic, but also create! In this part, we'll explore how Generative AI is revolutionizing various domains, from crafting stories to generating lifelike visuals.

Chapter 6: Unleashing the Power of Text Generation

Get ready to witness the magic of text generation! In this chapter, we'll delve into how AI can craft compelling narratives and explore the ethical considerations surrounding this technology.

- **Crafting Stories and Poems with Recurrent Neural Networks (RNNs):**

Remember RNNs from Part 1? They come back into play here! By analyzing massive amounts of text data, RNNs can learn the patterns and styles of different writing genres. This empowers them to generate creative text formats like poems, scripts, or even news articles.

- **The Ethics of Deepfakes: Exploring Text-to-Speech Synthesis:** Generative AI can also create realistic-sounding speech from text. This technology, known as text-to-speech synthesis, has immense potential for audiobooks and assistive technologies. However, its ability to mimic real voices raises ethical concerns, particularly around the creation of deepfakes — fabricated videos or audio recordings that appear real. We'll explore the potential dangers of deepfakes and discuss responsible development practices.

- **Applications of Text Generative AI: From Chatbots to Creative Writing:** The applications of text generation are vast. AI-powered chatbots can have more engaging conversations, while marketing

tools can personalize content for different

audiences. Writers can use generative

models to overcome writer's block or

brainstorm new ideas. The possibilities

are truly endless!

Chapter 7: Revolutionizing Visual Media with Generative AI

Get ready to have your mind blown by the world of generative AI for images and videos! In this chapter, we'll explore how AI can create stunning visuals and delve into the practical applications of this technology.

- **Deep Dream and Neural Style Transfer: Reimagining the World Through Artistic Filters:** Imagine applying artistic styles of famous painters like Van Gogh or Picasso to your photographs. This is the magic of Deep Dream and Neural Style Transfer algorithms! These generative models can transform images into works of art, inspiring creativity and visual exploration.

- **Building Realistic Images and Videos:** Generative AI is pushing the boundaries of image and video creation. AI models can now create entirely new, photorealistic images of people, landscapes, or even objects that have never existed before. Similarly, they can generate realistic videos, opening doors for new applications in filmmaking and animation.

- **Applications of Image/Video Generative AI: From Art Creation to Special Effects in Films:** The applications of generative AI in visual media are diverse. It can be used for creating concept art for films, generating special effects that would be too expensive or dangerous to film traditionally, or even personalizing marketing materials with unique visuals. As this technology matures, we can expect even more transformative applications to emerge.

This part has provided a glimpse into the exciting potential of Generative AI across various domains. We've explored how AI can craft captivating stories, generate realistic speech, and create stunning visuals. As generative AI continues to evolve, it promises to revolutionize the way we interact with information, create art, and experience the world around us.

Part 4: The Future Landscape of Generative AI

Chapter 8: Navigating the Ethical Labyrinth

As we stand on the precipice of a generative AI revolution, it's crucial to address the ethical considerations that accompany this powerful technology. This chapter will explore the challenges of bias, transparency, and responsible development in generative AI.

- **Mitigating Bias: Ensuring Fairness and Transparency in Generative AI:**

Generative models are only as good as the data they're trained on. Biased data can lead to biased outputs. We'll discuss strategies to mitigate bias in training data, promote fairness in generated content, and ensure transparency in how these models work.

- **Societal Impact and Responsible Development of Generative AI:** The widespread adoption of generative AI will undoubtedly impact society in profound ways. We'll explore potential concerns like job displacement due to automation, the spread of misinformation through deepfakes, and the potential for misuse of this technology. By fostering open discussions and establishing ethical guidelines, we can ensure that generative AI is developed and used responsibly for the benefit of society.

Chapter 9: Envisioning the Future of Generative AI

The future of generative AI is brimming with possibilities! In this chapter, we'll delve into cutting-edge research and explore the unforeseen applications and societal implications of this rapidly evolving field.

- **Research Frontiers: Pushing the Boundaries of Generative Models:**

Researchers are constantly pushing the boundaries of generative models. We'll explore exciting new architectures, the integration of other AI subfields like natural language processing and computer vision, and the potential for generative models to learn and adapt over time.

. **The Limitless Potential of Generative AI: Unforeseen Applications and Societal Implications:** The potential applications of generative AI extend far beyond what we can currently imagine. It could revolutionize fields like drug discovery, materials science, and personalized education. We'll explore potential societal implications, such as the creation of entirely new forms of art and entertainment, and the challenges of navigating a world where the line between reality and simulation can become increasingly blurred.

As we conclude our exploration of generative AI, it's clear that this technology holds immense potential to shape our future. By

fostering responsible development,

navigating ethical considerations, and

embracing the power of human creativity

alongside machine learning, we can ensure

that generative AI becomes a force for good

in the world.